A New Heart for XENA

WRITTEN BY
Mushy Crowley

ILLUSTRATED BY
SHERRY TRULL

To order additional copies of this book, contact:
Xlibris
844-714-8691
www.Xlibris.com
Orders@Xlibris.com

ISBN: Softcover   978-1-4535-5642-9
       Hardcover   978-1-4535-5643-6
       EBook   978-1-6698-2375-9

Library of Congress Control Number: 2010911759

Print information available on the last page

Rev. date: 04/30/2022

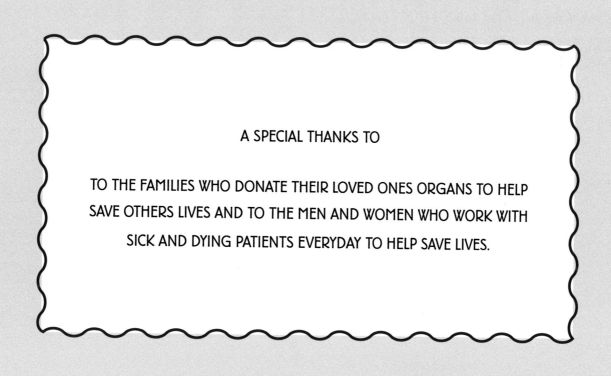

A SPECIAL THANKS TO

TO THE FAMILIES WHO DONATE THEIR LOVED ONES ORGANS TO HELP
SAVE OTHERS LIVES AND TO THE MEN AND WOMEN WHO WORK WITH
SICK AND DYING PATIENTS EVERYDAY TO HELP SAVE LIVES.

XENA WAS A LITTLE GIRL FROM A VERY SMALL TOWN. SHE LIVED WITH HER MOTHER, FATHER AND HER DOG NAMED JULIE. SHE LOVED PLAYING OUTSIDE WITH JULIE.

ONE DAY IT WAS TIME TO START SCHOOL. XENA WAS SO HAPPY WHEN HER MOTHER TOOK HER TO SCHOOL. SHE HAD HER NEW PINK AND PURPLE BACKPACK. SHE MET SO MANY NEW FRIENDS AND HER TEACHER WAS SO NICE.

5

AFTER SCHOOL ONE DAY, XENA BECAME VERY
SICK. HER MOTHER TOOK HER TO THE DOCTOR.
HER DOCTOR SAID, "XENA WILL NEED TO GO TO
THE HOSPITAL BECAUSE HER HEART IS REAL SICK."

WHILE SHE WAS IN THE HOSPITAL, MANY DOCTORS LOOKED AT XENA'S HEART. SHE HAD LOTS OF PICTURES MADE OF HER HEART.

THE DOCTOR TOLD XENA'S MOTHER AND DADDY THAT HER HEART WAS TOO SICK. XENA WOULD NEED TO GET A NEW HEART.

XENA WONDERED WHERE SHE WOULD GET A NEW HEART. MAYBE HER DADDY COULD BUILD HER ONE IN HIS SHOP,

9

OR MAYBE SHE COULD BUY ONE IN A STORE.

XENA'S MOTHER TOLD HER, "SOMEONE
WILL HAVE TO GIVE YOU THEIR HEART."
XENA WAITED AND WAITED IN THE
HOSPITAL FOR A NEW HEART, BUT NO
ONE HAD ONE TO GIVE.

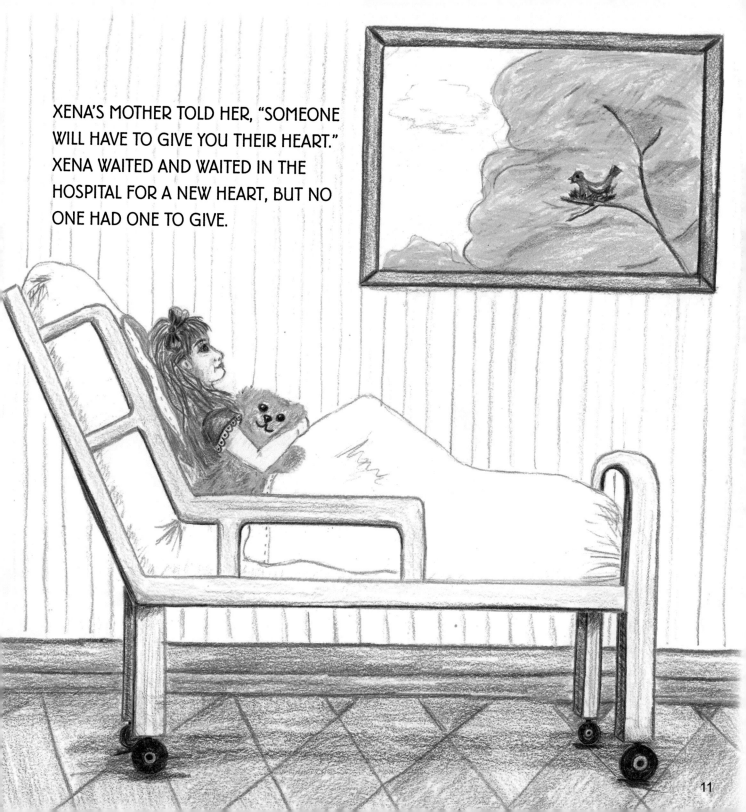

THEN ONE DAY, A LITTLE BOY WAS GOING TO LIVE WITH JESUS AND ASKED JESUS IF XENA COULD HAVE HIS HEART. HE SAID, "SINCE I AM GOING TO LIVE IN HEAVEN WITH YOU, I WILL NOT NEED MY HEART ANYMORE." JESUS WAS VERY PLEASED AND GAVE XENA THE HEART.

CHILDREN'S H

XENA HAD TO GO TO SURGERY TO GET THE NEW HEART. SHE HAD TO STAY IN THE HOSPITAL FOR A LONG TIME. MANY OF HER FRIENDS AND FAMILY CAME TO SEE HER. SHE GOT LOTS OF CARDS FROM AROUND THE COUNTRY.

Get Well

MANY PEOPLE PRAYED AND PRAYED THAT SHE WOULD GET BETTER.
PEOPLE ALSO PRAYED FOR THE LITTLE BOY WHO GAVE UP HIS HEART.

JESUS WAS VERY HAPPY ABOUT ALL THE PRAYERS.

WHEN XENA FELT BETTER, SHE WAS ABLE TO LEAVE THE HOSPITAL BUT HAD TO STAY IN AN APARTMENT CLOSE TO THE HOSPITAL. THE DOCTORS SAID THAT SHE WAS TOO SICK TO GO BACK TO HER SMALL TOWN.

XENA'S GRANDMOTHER SHELBY CAME TO STAY IN THE APARTMENT WITH HER. XENA WAS VERY EXCITED. HER GRANDMOTHER SHELBY PLAYED GAMES AND COOKED HER FAVORITE FOODS LIKE HOMEMADE POTATO SOUP. SHE LOVED THAT HER GRANDMOTHER SHELBY WAS STAYING WITH HER.

ONE DAY THE DOCTORS TOLD
XENA SHE COULD GO HOME TO
HER SMALL TOWN AND SEE ALL
HER FRIENDS AND HER LITTLE
DOG JULIE.

ON A SUNNY SATURDAY MORNING, XENA PACKED HER SUITCASE AND WAS ON HER WAY. BEFORE SHE GOT TO HER HOUSE, SHE SAW ALL OF HER FRIENDS ON THE SIDE OF THE ROAD WITH LOTS OF YELLOW BALLOONS.

AS THE CAR DROVE BY, XENA COULD SEE A BIG SIGN THAT SAID,

"WELCOME HOME XENA"

XENA ASKED HER MOTHER, "ARE THOSE PEOPLE WITH THOSE PRETTY BALLOONS HERE TO SEE ME?" "YES!" HER MOTHER AND FATHER SAID.

"EVERYONE IS HAPPY YOU ARE HOME!"

XENA WAS SO HAPPY TO SEE EVERYONE. AS SHE DROVE BY, ALL THE PRETTY BALLOONS WAS RELEASED IN THE SKY.

AS THE BALLOONS WERE FLOWING INTO THE SKY, THE LITTLE
BOY WHO GAVE HIS HEART CAUGHT ONE.

ON THE END OF THE BALLOON THEIR WAS A MESSAGE THAT READ.

THANK YOU JESUS
XENA HAS A NEW
HEART!

SINCE XENA RECEIVED HER NEW HEART IN 2008, SHE IS BACK

AT SCHOOL WITH ALL HER FRIENDS. SHE STILL LOVES PLAYING

WITH HER DOG JULIE AND IS HELPING RAISE MONEY FOR

ORGAN DONATION AWARNESS.

Printed in the United States
by Baker & Taylor Publisher Services